SYMBOLIC
FENG SHUI
& AMAZING CRYSTALS

'SARVSHRI' Dr. NITIN PARAKH
B.E. CIVIL (Hons.), C. Eng. (I), AMIE, AIV, DBM, Ph. D.
Chartered Engineer, Approved Valuer. (Gold Medallist)
and
MRS. SEEMA PARAKH
B.A. (Psychology)

NAVNEET PUBLICATIONS (INDIA) LIMITED

Price : Rs. 50.00   G 082 | S 661

Second Edition : September, 2002.

NAVNEET PUBLICATIONS (INDIA) LIMITED

Bhavani Shankar Road, Dadar, Mumbai - 400 028.

e-mail : npil@navneet.com

Website : www.navneet.com • www.connectschool.com

Disclaimer : This book describes information & techniques, which have been used throughout the orient for many years. The information detailed in this book, is to the author's and co-author's best knowledge and experiences, and are no claims for their absolute effectiveness. They are to be used by the readers at their own discretion & liability. It may or may not be beneficial depending on one's stage of development. The use of the material offered in this book is totally at the reader's own responsibility and the author, co-author, publisher and printer of this book are not responsible or liable in any manner whatsoever.

ISBN : 81-243-0891-8

Published by Navneet Publications (I) Ltd., Dantali, Gujarat.

Printed at : Paramount Litho & Offset Works, Mumbai - 400 011.

Tel. : 091-22-515 0265
Fax : 091-22-510 4458

**K. J. SOMAIYA COMPREHENSIVE COLLEGE OF EDUCATION
TRAINING & RESEARCH**
(Adhyapak Mahavidyalaya)
Vidyavihar, Ghatkopar (E), Mumbai-400 077.

SMT. SOUDAMINI C. MENON
I/C. Principal

Ref. No. K/ 95 /2002.
Date : 18-03-2002.

Dr. Nitin Parakh,
Juhu,
MUMBAI.

Sub : Appreciation of your good work.

Dear Dr. Parakh,

This is to inform you that after taking
Fengshui Consultation from you, our college has
experienced a lot of improvement and benefit.
I really appreciate your help, co-operation and
good work, tremendously. My whole staff also joins me
in thanking you from the bottom of their hearts.

May God bless you.

Regards,

Yours sincerely,

(SMT. SOUDAMINI C. MENON)
I/C. Principal.

iii

T E S T I M O N I A L

To:
Dr. Nitin Parakh,
Fengshui & Vaastu Consultant,
Mumbai.

Dear Sir,

Your visit to my house, office and shops for Fengshui audits was more than a year back. Thinking of that day and as on today – what a world of difference !

Being a bit unfortunate and bundled with a lot of problems, your advice has immensely changed my life for the good ! I thank you very much for the timely guidance and authentic advice. My floral business and my chemical business, both have been benefited immensely. The promotion I am getting and the work people have appreciated is very well seen in the 20th May 2002 issue of a well known Gujarati magazine – 'Chitralekha'.

May your kind and fruitful consultation bring a lot of happiness and peace amongst those unfortunate ones and make a world a better place to live. Thanks once again and may God bless you always !

Yours truly,

Nalini S. Kapadia
Mumbai

39/1013, Adarsh Nagar, Prabhdevi, Mumbai - 400 025. ℗ 432 49 02 Fax :432 30 91 Shop:380 40 64 Email : may_flower@mail.com

B. K. Vatsaraj

CHARTERED ACCOUNTANT

201 - B, Express Apartments,

Yari Road, Versova,

Mumbai - 400 061.

Tel. : 631 03 23 / 639 24 62

April 16, 2002

To

Nitin Parakh,

Feng Shui Master,

Mumbai

Dear Sir,

I am a chartered accountant and my wife Dr. Jyoti is a Dentist. I had invited you for feng shui audits for my office and my wife's clinic in the year 1999 after reading your interview in 'Times of India'. I express my heartfelt and sincere gratitude to you, because after your visits, both mine and my wife's professional practices have improved tremendously! In fact I am a much sought after Chartered Accountant today, and my sincere and honest work in now greatly appreciated by all my clients.

May god bless you with a very long life and you continue to help people lead a much better life.

Yours Sincerely,

B. K. Vatsaraj

(Raju Vatsaraj)

Tel. :+91-22-612 5875 (4 Lines) • Fax :+91-91-613 4924

Office : Fort Chambers, 'C' Block, 65, Tamarind Lane, 1st Floor, Fort, Mumbai - 400 023. • Tel. : +91-22-265 39 31 • Email : bkvat@yahoo.com

DETAILS OF PROFESSIONAL FENG SHUI QUALIFICATIONS OF DR. NITIN PARAKH

1. Graduated in the highly prestigious 'MASTER PRACTITIONER COURSE' from Lillian Too Institute of Feng Shui' at Malaysia.

2. Qualified in the advanced 'PRACTITIONER'S LEVEL 1 COURSE' from the 'Wind & Water Geomancy Centre', Singapore.

3. Studied the 'XUAN KONG FENG SHUI COURSE' - Flying Stars (all 4 units) from 'Yap Cheng Hai Feng Shui Centre of Excellence', Malaysia.

4. Studied ELEMENTARY, INTERMEDIATE AND ADVANCED level Flying Star Feng Shui Courses from Master Joseph Yu's Feng Shui Research Centre, Canada.

5. Qualified in advanced level FLYING STAR FENG SHUI after completing the prestigious 'MASTER CLASS' with Master Joseph Yu, the world's leading authority on FLYING STAR FENG SHUI.

6. One of the few illustrious individuals of the world to be awarded the extremely prestigious 'HIGHER DIPLOMA IN FENG SHUI' by Master Joseph Yu-Canada, after passing the examinations.

7. 'Sarvshri' Dr. Nitin Parakh is one of the few select individuals of the world to receive official recognition as 'FENG SHUI PRACTITIONER' from the Feng Shui Research Centre, Canada, after passing the exams.

8. Completed the workshop on 'GEOPATHIC STRESS' conducted by Master Healer 'Christan Hummel' – INSTITUTE OF METAPHYSICAL STUDIES (USA).

9. Member of the 'FENG SHUI SOCIETY' London (U.K.)

DETAILS OF PROFESSIONAL FENG SHUI QUALIFICATIONS OF MRS. SEEMA PARAKH

1. Completed the course 'PRACTICAL FENG SHUI FOR MODERN LIVING' conducted by the 'Wind & Water Geomancy Centre', Singapore.

2. Qualified in the advanced 'PRACTITIONER'S LEVEL 1 COURSE' from the 'Wind & Water Geomancy Centre', Singapore.

3. Received training for many years under her husband, Sarvshri DR. NITIN PARAKH, India's leading Feng Shui Master & the country's top level authority on 'FLYING STARS FENG SHUI' & 'EIGHT MANSIONS FENG SHUI'.

4. Completed the workshop on 'GEOPATHIC STRESS' conducted by Master Healer 'Christan Hummel' – INSTITUTE OF METAPHYSICAL STUDIES, (USA)

Sarvshri DR. NITIN PARAKH with Master LILLIAN TOO during the days of MASTER PRACTITIONER COURSE. Dr. Parakh graduated in Feng Shui at Lillian Too's Institute of Feng Shui, where he had led his group from the front to win the 'FIRST PRIZE' in the FENG SHUI COMPETITION at Kuala Lumpur, Malaysia.

Sarvshri DR. NITIN PARAKH receiving his Certificate after completing the prestigious 'MASTER CLASS' in advance level FLYING STAR FENG SHUI, from his Si Fu, MASTER JOSEPH YU.

Sarvshri DR. NITIN PARAKH lecturing on Feng Shui at the 'LIONS CLUB' of Bombay Uptown, where he was invited and honoured as the 'CHIEF GUEST'.

Mrs. Seema Parakh lecturing on Feng Shui, to the members of 'EXPERIMENT IN INTERNATIONAL LIVING' Bombay Centre, where she was invited as the 'CHIEF GUEST'.

PREFACE

It is my firm conviction that most readers have already read my best-seller 'FENG SHUI - 80 Golden Ways To Good Luck', which is available in English, Hindi, Marathi, Gujarati, Bengali, Telugu, Malayalam and Tamil.

'FENG SHUI - 80 Golden Ways To Good Luck' describes easy measures to enhance fortunes of the house and also deals with some most common Feng Shui materials. Since its publication, I have received letters from many readers asking me to write about more materials useful in Feng Shui. Some readers have also asked me to clarify and elaborate on some of the items described in the earlier book, like the three-legged frog, the horseshoe, etc. I have done precisely that and much more in the first part of this book. This part also describes a lot of other useful symbolic Feng Shui cures and auspicious Feng Shui dimensions.

The second part of this book deals with the amazing power of crystals and describes the various types of crystals which even a layman can use easily to bring luck to his life. Actually this is not just one book, but two books in one !

Mumbai

15th August, 2002

(Dr. Nitin Parakh)

This Book Is Dedicated
With All My Love
To My Loving Sisters
Manisha & Tina
& My Lovely Daughters
Kanika & Anushka

CONTENTS

A | SYMBOLIC FENG SHUI - An Introduction

Feng Shui is a Chinese Science that has gained immense popularity in recent years due to its ease of implementation and tremendous effectiveness.

The Chinese people have a great penchant for looking at objects and symbols as conveyors of hidden meanings. They look at many objects as conveyors of symbolic good luck or bad luck and they also view many events as omens of good or bad luck.

Objects and pictures are said to contain much more meaning than is visible at first. Hidden meanings attached to objects and events have much greater potency that words cannot describe! For example, if one puts up in one's house, a picture of a family with a crying woman, along with a man wearing old torn clothes, it clearly symbolizes ill luck! The hidden meaning would be that the man, who represents the breadwinner, is in dire poverty hence it indicates financial bad luck, and also the mourning woman may indicate death of a dear one or sadness due to some other reason. Hence, putting up such a picture is symbolic of inviting poverty and sadness into the home!

On the other hand, a happy family photograph showing a family of father, mother and children all close together, smiling and happy and the lady of the house wearing a lot of jewellery, symbolizes a lot of good luck indicating good wealth luck, good descendants' luck, as well as happiness and togetherness. Such a picture is auspicious for displaying in the house and invariably brings good tidings. This is how the Chinese people look at pictures and objects. This is symbolic Feng Shui! Strictly speaking, symbolic Feng Shui is actually traditional Chinese cultural Symbolism.

The Chinese people traditionally use a large number of Symbols in their house. There are Symbols and objects for enhancement of good luck for Health, Wealth, Success, Marriage prospects and Good relationship. These have been described in detail in the following chapter.

▲ ▲ ▲

<table>
<tr><td>B</td><td>THE VARIOUS FENG SHUI
SYMBOLS FOR GOOD LUCK</td></tr>
</table>

AUSPICIOUS DIMENSIONS FOR GOOD LUCK

In Symbolic Feng Shui, it is believed that certain dimensions are auspicious and bring good luck, whereas certain dimensions are inauspicious and bring bad luck. Hence, when you make new furniture or renovate your office or house, make the tables, chairs, etc. according to the auspicious dimensions to create Good luck Chi for you !

As such all the furniture in the house and office have lucky and unlucky dimensions. The table, chair, cupboard, etc. can be measured with the help of a Feng Shui ruler. You can check whether the dimensions are auspicious or inauspicious.

The Feng Shui ruler has eight cycles of dimensions out of which four are auspicious and four are inauspicious. The measure of each cycle is equal to 17 inches or 43 cms and each cycle is divided into eight portions. The cycle of auspicious and inauspicious dimensions repeats itself over and over again to infinity. Once you get accustomed with the use of Feng Shui dimensions, you can use it for any kind of furniture.

It can even be used for designing auspicious visiting cards, envelopes, etc.

THE FOUR AUSPICIOUS DIMENSIONS

1. **Chai** – This dimension is between 0 inches and $2\frac{1}{8}$ inches or 5.4 cms. This is the first portion of the cycle and it is divided into four categories of good luck. The first approximate half inch brings money luck, the second brings jewellery, the third brings six types of good luck and the fourth brings abundance.

2. **Yi** – This dimension is between $6\frac{3}{8}$ inches and $8\frac{1}{2}$ inches or in cms it is between 16.2 cms and 21.5 cms. This is the fourth section of the cycle. It enhances mentor luck, i.e. it brings helpful people into your life. This also has four sub-divisions. The first $\frac{1}{2}$ inch brings excellent children luck, the second gets unexpected income, the third predicts a very successful son and the fourth brings excellent good fortune.

3. **Kwan** – This dimension is between $8\frac{1}{2}$ inches and $10\frac{5}{8}$ inches or 21.5 cms to 27 cms. This is the fifth section of the cycle and brings power luck. The first $\frac{1}{2}$ inch means easy to pass exams, the second brings special luck, the third improves income and the fourth brings high honours for the family.

4. **Pun** – This dimension is between $14\frac{7}{8}$ to 17 inches or 37.5 cms to 43.2 cms. The first sub-section increases money flow, the second brings examination luck, the third jewellery and the fourth a lot of prosperity.

THE FOUR INAUSPICIOUS DIMENSIONS

1. **Pi** — This dimension is between $2\frac{1}{8}$ to $4\frac{2}{8}$ inches or 5.4 cms to 10.8 cms. This dimension brings bad luck especially illnesses. The first $\frac{1}{2}$ inch means money flow becomes less and less, the second indicates legal problems, the third brings bad luck which can even send you to jail, and the fourth refers to death of either of the spouse.

2. **Li** — This dimension is between $4\frac{2}{8}$ to $6\frac{3}{8}$ inches or 10.8 cms. to 16.2 cms. This category leads to separation. The first $\frac{1}{2}$ inch brings a host of bad luck, the second predicts losing money, the third means you will meet unscrupulous people and the fourth means loss of everything or being plundered totally.

3. **Chieh** — This dimension is between $10\frac{5}{8}$ to $12\frac{6}{8}$ inches or 27 cms to 32.4 cms. This dimension refers to loss. The first $\frac{1}{2}$ inch means death, the second means that all that you need will disappear and you could lose your livelihood. The third brings total disgrace, and the fourth indicates a huge loss of money.

4. **Hai** — This dimension is between $12\frac{6}{8}$ to $14\frac{7}{8}$ inches or 32.4 cms to 37.5 cms. These dimensions indicate extreme bad luck. The first refers to disasters, the second death, the third sickness and the fourth scandal and quarrels.

The 8 parts of each cycle of these dimensions keep repeating itself in the same manner infinitely.

To summarise and to simplify, the following table

lists out the lucky dimensions. The way to use it is simple, e.g. when you make a new office table, keep the length, breadth as well as the height within the range of one of the set of auspicious dimensions listed below :

Auspicious dimensions

$0''$	to	$2\frac{1}{8}''$
$6\frac{3}{8}''$	to	$8\frac{1}{2}''$
$8\frac{1}{2}''$	to	$10\frac{5}{8}''$
$14\frac{7}{8}''$	to	$17''$
$17''$	to	$19\frac{1}{8}''$
$23\frac{3}{8}''$	to	$25\frac{1}{2}''$
$25\frac{1}{2}''$	to	$27\frac{5}{8}''$
$31\frac{7}{8}''$	to	$34''$
$34''$	to	$36\frac{1}{8}''$
$40\frac{3}{8}''$	to	$42\frac{1}{2}''$
$42\frac{1}{2}''$	to	$44\frac{5}{8}''$
$48\frac{7}{8}''$	to	$51''$
$51''$	to	$53\frac{1}{8}''$
$57\frac{3}{8}''$	to	$59\frac{1}{2}''$
$59\frac{1}{2}''$	to	$61\frac{5}{8}''$
$65\frac{7}{8}''$	to	$68''$
$68''$	to	$70\frac{1}{8}''$

As a practical example an office-table of 32" height, 26" width and 50" length, would be very lucky because all its dimensions fall within the range of the auspicious dimensions as per the above chart.

Auspicious Visiting Cards

You may even design your visiting card as per these auspicious dimensions. A visiting card is used by people to convey information about themselves, it acts as your ambassador to bring in prospective business. Hence, it is a good idea to have a visiting card as per the auspicious dimensions.

A practical example of an auspicious-sized visiting card is a card of height 2" as well as width 2". It may appear a bit small but it can help in bringing you good luck! Those readers who do not have too much information required to be printed on their visiting cards, should make their cards of this size to enhance their luck. I am unable to do it myself because of too much information on my visiting card, but then of course I have the tremendously powerful Flying Stars and Eight Mansion Feng Shui already helping me anyway !

WISH-GRANTING COW

The cow is considered as a holy animal in India and Nepal. People here worship the cow and this animal holds a special place in the hearts of people. In Feng Shui, the wish-fulfilling cow is symbolic of good descendants' luck.

Wish-Granting Cow

Very few people actually know the true significance of the cow. In fact, Buddhism teaches us that the cow has the power to transform our wishes into reality if we treat it with kindness, and also if we do not eat beef (cow's meat).

In an office, to enhance good fortune you can display the cow sitting on a bed of coins and ingots anywhere on your desk. At home you can display the wish-granting cow in the South East sector of your house. This can be very lucky since South East is the general sector which is associated with wealth. You can even hang a painting of a cow in the South East sector to energise wealth luck.

As the name suggests the wish-granting cow is symbolic of a person's wishes being fulfilled. It should only be used by people who do not consume beef (cow's meat).

PAGODA / EDUCATION TOWER

The pagoda or the education tower is said to possess certain powers which helps to transform unruly minds into well-disciplined minds. It is a good enhancer for those who wish to achieve academic success.

The Chinese Pagoda has evolved from the Buddhist stupa, which is considered as a sacred object. You can place a pagoda in a child's room to increase his/her concentration in studies and also to reduce his/her boisterous behaviour.

The pagoda is said to have the power to keep away anything that could distract the mind. It is very useful for children with distractive minds and for those who lack proper concentration.

Pagoda

The best place to keep the pagoda is the North East corner of the child's bedroom. The pagoda is considered to have **yin** energy, and so as to make it effective, it should be balanced by **yang** energy in the room, i.e. by having red colour present in the room. The yang effect of the red colour helps to awaken the **chi** of the pagoda.

CHI LIN

The Chi Lin is a mythical animal or a Chinese Unicorn. It is also known as a Dragon Horse since it has the head of a dragon and the body of a horse.

The Chi Lin is a fantastic symbol of prosperity, success, longevity, illustrious offspring, etc. It brings sons. It is associated with the *He-tu* square which is used in advanced Feng Shui. The Chi Lin is supposed to have emerged from the yellow river with the mystical map on its back. It is said to have magical qualities.

The presence of the Chi Lin attracts the cosmic breath of the dragon, which brings a lot of good fortune with it. The dragon horse can be displayed in the house in the living room near the vicinity of the main door. But it should not face the main door directly.

Chi Lin

The Chi Lin is very lucky for those wanting promotions or advancements in their careers. It is also very fortunate for those working in the military, since the Chi Lin is a symbol of the first rank military official. It is considered very auspicious to display the Chi Lin at the workplace. It can be placed on the office desk to enhance prosperity.

The Chi Lin is also used as a cure for some flying star afflictions. The Chi Lin should be made of brass and should be placed in pairs.

DRAGON TURTLE

The Dragon Turtle is a Chinese legendary symbol. It is a combination of the dragon and the tortoise which are two of the four most important creatures of Chinese symbolism. The image of a Dragon turtle is such that it has the head of a dragon and the body of a turtle sitting on a bed of coins and ingots. It has a coin in its mouth and a baby tortoise on its back. It is an imaginary animal and the Chinese people use this symbol to enhance their houses and offices.

The tortoise symbolizes longevity whereas the dragon symbolizes success, courage and determination. It shows that the turtle has transformed into a dragon, which is indicative of good fortune in a person's career and business. The base on which the dragon turtle sits is made up of coins and ingots, which in turn represents abundant wealth and prosperity. The coin in its mouth signifies increased money flow.

There is a small baby tortoise on its back which is symbolic of excellent descendants'-luck which generally means many sons!

Dragon Turtle

You can place the dragon turtle either in the North or the East sector of your home. But in an office if these two sectors fall directly in front of your seat, you should not place the dragon turtle there. Try and place it by your side, i.e. parallel to where you sit. Another location to place the dragon turtle is right behind your seat but looking sideways. This signifies that you are getting the support of both the dragon and the turtle!

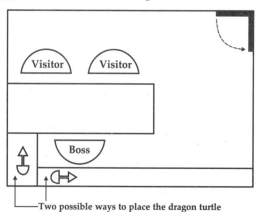

Two possible ways to place the dragon turtle

Ideal Ways to Place the Dragon Turtle in Office

Take care not to put this powerful symbol directly in front of you as it could invite many problems!

The sketch on page 26 shows two possible ways to place the dragon turtle, in your office. You may place it in one of the two positions.

(DOUBLE HAPPINESS SYMBOL)

One of the most powerful and widely recognized symbols for marital happiness is the Double Happiness Symbol.

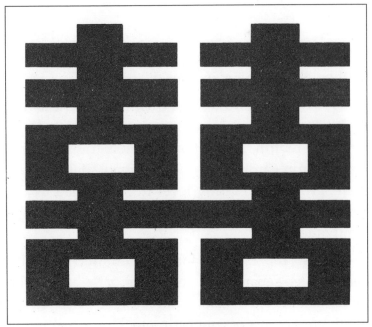

Double Happiness Symbol

This symbol is depicted in a bright red colour since red enhances love and romance in a person's life.

In China, this symbol is carved on chairs and bedroom furniture. It can also be printed on fabrics for dresses. The Double Happiness symbol signifies undying love. It can be placed under the mattress of the married couple. It can also be hung or displayed on the South West area of the bedroom.

The double happiness symbol is an easy and nice way to enhance relations with your spouse.

(MYSTIC KNOT)

The mystic knot is also called the love knot. It has neither the beginning and nor the end.

It is said to swallow its own tail. It reflects the Buddhist ideology that existence is an endless cycle of birth and rebirth. In spiritual tradition, this symbol is very often regarded as a lucky symbol, but at a less than spiritual or earthly level it is regarded as the perfect symbol of never ending love and unity amongst family members.

It also represents a long life uninterrupted by heartbreaks, separations, sufferings or setbacks. The mystic knot is red in colour and it can be placed in the South West corner of your bedroom. This enhances the

Mystic Knot

relationship of the couple. If you are looking at improving the relationship between family members, the mystic knot should be displayed in the South West corner of the living room. If placed in the South West of the office, it ensures harmony between the staff members and the boss. It symbolises that the employees will be loyal and the employer will be more considerate.

8

PI YAO

The Pi Yao is an auspicious creature of good fortune. It is used to overcome bad Feng Shui. The Pi Yao is extremely useful as a remedy for certain flying star problems. While carrying out renovations if you have offended the Grand Duke – Jupiter – you are sure to have bad luck immediately. You can place the Pi Yao in the affected corner to reduce the effects of the

bad luck caused by disturbing the Grand Duke —
Jupiter. The following paragraphs will make this
clearer.

Flying Star Feng Shui is a complex but, very very
accurate Science which helps to understand the general
luck of a house and to enhance it. The general Flying
Star chart of a house is made using data like the year
of construction of the house and its exact facing
direction. The Flying Star chart of a house is like a
horoscope of the house which tells exactly about the
general good luck or bad luck of the house and also
reveals the secrets of the lucky and unlucky locations
within the house. Apart from this, there is also

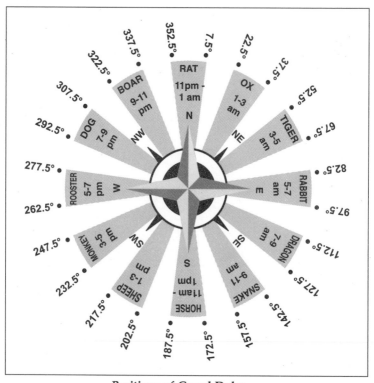

Positions of Grand Duke

something called Annual Flying Stars which predict **small** changes in the luck of the various rooms of a house during each year. Annual Flying Stars also reveal about the time-taboos for renovation. Most people are unaware of the fact that if they break or do partial structure-renovations in some part of their house during certain years they tend to disturb a time-taboo, and this causes bad luck, sometimes quite severely! Time-taboos for renovations are valid only if you renovate a house where you are already living. These taboos do not apply to the structural renovations which you do in a house, before you actually move into it. In a nutshell, all these suggest that if you are thinking of a major renovation of a particular room in your house, think again. Do it only after taking professional advice! Be careful as you might disturb one of the time-taboos for the year and invite bad luck.

One of the major time-taboos is the Grand Duke–Jupiter. The location of the Grand Duke–Jupiter changes every year. The following table tells where the Grand Duke is located during certain years. It only occupies 15° of the compass direction.

YEAR	RULING ANIMAL	LOCATION OF GRAND DUKE–JUPITER
2001	Snake	South - South East
2002	Horse	South
2003	Sheep	South - South West
2004	Monkey	West - South West
2005	Rooster	West
2006	Dog	West - North West

Pi Yao

Suppose you plan to renovate thoroughly (knocking the walls off, changing the place of doors, etc.) the 'South' room of your house in the year 2002. Then, you will be disturbing the Grand Duke and this can cause bad luck for up to 3 years. Hence, such a structural renovation is best avoided. But if you have already done it inadvertently, then, as a remedy you must place a pair of Pi Yao in that room to reduce the effect of disturbing the Grand Duke–Jupiter.

9

CALABASH

The Calabash is also known as the Ho Lu. It is a very powerful symbol of good fortune as well as longevity. The Calabash is shaped like a bottle gourd. It symbolizes the union of heaven and earth in miniature. The upper half is the heaven and the lower half is the earth. In fact, wealth vases are also shaped like the Calabash.

Calabash

You can display the real dried gourd in and around your home, which shows that your house is being blessed. The model of a Ho Lu can also be used but it should be made in brass only. It is mainly a cure for health-related problems caused by Flying Star afflictions. The Ho Lu should be placed near the bed of the sick person. Even the God of Longevity is shown to carry a staff with a bottle gourd containing the elixir of immortality hanging at its one end.

The Ho Lu / Calabash is an excellent way to remove/reduce the effects of the sickness star numeral '2' in Flying Star Feng Shui. It is also used in pairs generally. The Ho Lu should certainly be kept in your bedroom during the years when the Annual Flying Star '2' is in your bedroom location.

The location of the Annual Sickness Star '2' during

a particular year is shown by the following table :

YEAR	POSITIONS OF ANNUAL FLYING STAR '2'
2001	North East
2002	South
2003	North
2004	South West
2005	East
2006	South East

A practical example demonstrating the use of the above table is as follows :

If your bedroom is, say, in the South Zone of your house, then, in the year 2002 the Annual Flying Star 2, which causes illness, is in your room. Hence, to reduce its effect, you should place a pair of Ho Lu/ Calabash near your bed, all through the year 2002. During the year 2003, the Annual Sickness Star '2' will be in the North room of your house, hence the pair of Ho Lu should be shifted to that room in 2003. Please note that for Flying Star calculations, generally, the Chinese Year period is considered from 5th Feb. of that year to 4th Feb. of the subsequent year. E.g. the year 2002 refers to the period between 5th Feb. 2002 up to 4th Feb. 2003 of the English Calendar.

During the years when the Annual Sickness Star '2' is in a location of your house where there is a toilet or a store room, you need not worry, and the use of the Ho Lu as a cure for the Annual Sickness Star '2', is only required whenever the Annual Sickness Star '2', comes to a sector of your house, where there is a bedroom.

DOUBLE FISH SYMBOL

The double fish symbol is symbolic of sexual unions and also successful partnerships. It also symbolizes harmony and unity in the family. In a house, the best place to display a double fish symbol is the dining area where the whole family sits together for a meal. It is also a protective symbol and enhances auspicious Chi.

This symbol is regarded as one of the eight treasures of Buddha. It creates energies which help in keeping the married couple together and thus reducing the number of divorces.

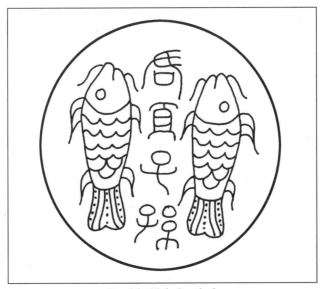

Double Fish Symbol

ARROWANA FISH

The word fish, in Feng Shui is regarded as abundant wealth. So different kinds of fishes are used to create energies that enhance good fortune and bring in riches.

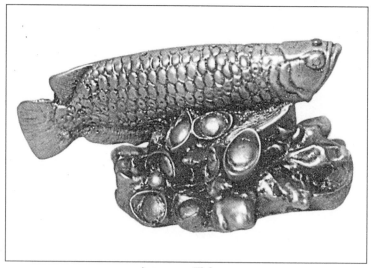

Arrowana Fish

The Chinese refer to the Arrowana fish as the Feng Shui fish. You can keep live Arrowana fish in an aquarium in your office or at home. The scales of the Arrowana should be shining and should show a tinge of either pink, gold or silver. If you keep a dull Arrowana it will not be so effective. Instead of the live fish you can even place the model of the Arrowana fish.

The Arrowana is also called the dragon fish and the most auspicious area to place it is the North, or East or South East sector of your office or house.

DISPLAY THE HORSE

The horse is a majestic animal and it signifies nobility. It is **yang** in nature. In symbolic Feng Shui, it is used as one of the best methods to bring victory luck. A tribute horse is shown as a white horse laden with gifts. You can put up a painting or picture of a tribute horse, but the colour of the horse should be white. In the picture, the horse should be shown as being led by an official and not mounted.

It is not advisable to display a horse that is raring up, especially if it is directly behind you or directly in front of you. This can lead to accidents involving damage to your limbs.

Displaying the white tribute horse is very auspicious as it symbolizes upward mobility and promotion. The best location to place the horse is the living room and in the South corner. Do not display the horse in any of the bedrooms. Similarly, in an office you can place the horse in the South sector.

13

PAIR OF ELEPHANTS

The elephant is considered as a sacred animal in many countries. Especially in India, the Hindus worship Lord Ganesh who is depicted as an elephant-headed God. In symbolic Feng Shui, the elephant is regarded as a lucky symbol for fertility and descendant luck. A childless couple who wishes to have a baby can place a pair of elephants in their bedroom next to the bed.

The elephant also symbolises good fortune. It is very auspicious to place a pair of elephants near your main door either inside or outside. You can place a basket containing precious things on the back of the elephants. This is symbolic of prosperity and wealth coming your way.

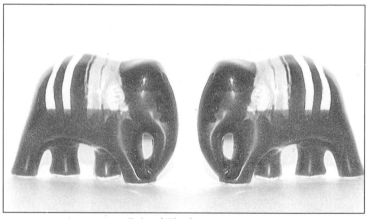

Pair of Elephants

THE MONGOOSE

The mongoose is another animal that symbolizes getting wealth as well as overcoming bad luck. The mongoose is shown as sitting on a bed of gold ingots and coins. It is said to give out jewels and gem stones from its mouth. **The mongoose looks like the rat.** It can be placed on your office desk to enhance wealth luck and to reduce the bad Feng Shui of your place. In the home, you can display the mongoose in the living room as an energizer for more jewellery and riches coming into your house.

Mongoose

LAUGHING BUDDHA AND KUAN YIN BUDDHA

The Laughing Buddha is regarded as one of the gods of wealth. It brings prosperity, success and financial gains to the house. The location of placing the Laughing Buddha is important. It has to be placed at some 30" approximate height and should be facing the main door directly. The energy that enters the house from the main door is greeted by the Laughing Buddha and the energy is activated, and turns highly prosperous. If this location is not possible, the next best place to keep the Laughing Buddha, is on a side table, or a corner table which is diagonally opposite to the

Laughing Buddha

front door and facing the door. It is not advisable to keep the Laughing Buddha in the bedroom or in the dining room. This god of wealth is not worshipped or prayed to, but just displayed, as its presence is purely symbolic and auspicious.

I want to clarify here that many forms of the Laughing Buddha are available, some in the standing position, some in the sitting position. All are fine, but the sitting position one, with a bag of money behind him, is better among all the forms.

Another very popular energizer for wealth and prosperity are the Lucky Charm cards. These Lucky Charm cards can be placed in a person's wallet, purse or pocket. The Laughing Buddha Charm Cards symbolize happiness, wealth and good luck. Another type of Lucky Charm Card normally used is the Kuan yin Buddha Charm Card which is the symbol of safety and protection. It is quite a useful one for people engaged in hazardous professions like pilots, sailors, etc.

MERCHANT SHIP WITH GOLD INGOTS

In China, a merchant ship filled with gold coins and ingots was a very popular and widely used symbol for business success. The shape of a model ship is like that of a dragon with merchants or traders sitting in it and is filled with cargo and gold ingots. This is a very auspicious symbol. You can place such a ship in your office or home. The ship should be placed in such a manner that it is sailing into the harbour. Here, the harbour means your home or office.

Merchant Ship with Gold Ingots

The merchant ship is a very good energizer for bringing in wealth. The Chinese people display this ship, in order to achieve higher income and more business. But be careful while placing the ship, it should not be sailing outwards, since that would symbolize money going away rather than coming in!

17

(WEALTH VASE)

A wealth vase is considered to ensure the preservation and continuing growth of the family's wealth. A wealth vase can be made of porcelain, china or any pottery that you may like. The shape of the vase should be such that it has a wide mouth, a narrow neck, a fat body and stable flat base. If possible, the vase should have auspicious symbols like the dragon and the phoenix painted on it.

Fill up the vase up to the brim with the following objects and keep it hidden from general view :

▲ Seven types of semi-precious stones like crystals,

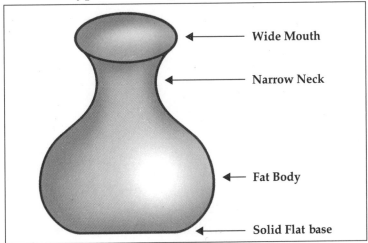

Ideal Wealth Vase

pearls, corals, jasper, lapis, cornelian, quartz, aquamarine, topaz, citrine, amethyst, tiger eye, etc.

▲ A little soil from a rich man's house. You should ask for it and not steal it. Soil that is given to you is very lucky for you.

▲ 3, 6, or 9 Chinese coins with red thread.

▲ A red packet filled with real money preferably a big denomination.

▲ 5 types of nourishing edibles, to signify plenty of food to eat at all times. This can be wheat, dates, barley, millet, soyabeans, red beans, sorghum. Place it in a small plastic bag and then into the wealth vase. These can be put directly without the plastic bag also.

You can place the wealth vase inside a cupboard, in your bedroom or living room, But it should be kept hidden from open view.

18

DRAGON

The dragon is a symbol of excellent **yang** energy. You can energize your office by keeping the model of a dragon on the East side of your office. The East is the direction associated with this celestial creature. The element of the East is wood, hence a dragon carved out of wood is very good. You can even use a dragon

Dragon

made of ceramic or crystal, but don't keep metal ones because metal destroys the wood element of the East. It is very good to display pictures of dragons in the East of restaurants, shops, departmental stores, etc. wherever a lot of **yang** energy and movement is desirable. Avoid the display of the dragon model or its pictures in the bedrooms because these are places where we intend to rest, and a symbol as **yang** as the dragon is not advisable there.

PHOENIX

The phoenix is an imaginary creature of the ancient Chinese Feng Shui. It is widely used in symbolic Feng

Phoenix

Shui. The phoenix is usually red or crimson in colour. It symbolises the luck of wish fulfilment. The South corner of your home or office can be activated by placing the phoenix there. The phoenix brings opportunities, fame and recognition. You can energise your luck by putting up pictures, painting an artificial model of the phoenix in the South area. The image of the phoenix at a distance also symbolizes far-sightedness which is essential for any intelligent businessman.

DRAGON AND PHOENIX TOGETHER

The dragon and the phoenix are two very powerful and important symbols of Chinese mythology. The dragon represents male vigour and fertility, whereas the phoenix represents female beauty. The dragon is considered to be very *yang* and brings in prosperity. Individually, the phoenix is a yang symbol but in the presence of the dragon it becomes *yin*.

The dragon and the phoenix together in a home symbolize a successful marriage, a great deal of prosperity and many offsprings. The union of these two wonderful creatures suggests a strong bonding between the couple in a marriage. It also brings in a lot of money and descendants' luck.

Dragon and Phoenix Together

The dragon represents the Patriarch whereas the phoenix represents the Matriarch. The model of the dragon and phoenix together can be placed·in the North-West sector to enhance the Patriarch's luck. If placed in the South-West area it enhances the luck of the matriarch and is a very good symbol for energizing relationships. The dragon and phoenix in the East improves the health of the family members and in the South it brings opportunities and recognition. Thus there are many places where you can keep this excellent symbol of good fortune, according to your personal requirement.

(THREE-LEGGED FROG/ TOAD)

The three-legged frog/toad is considered very lucky. It usually has one or three coins in its mouth. The position of the three-legged toad is important. It is best to place it somewhere near your main door discreetly on the floor or on a low shelf. It need not be seen. It can even be placed behind a couch near the main door. I personally advise to place it near the main door, on the inside, with the toad looking inwards, symbolizing money coming in. Some people advise that every morning when the breadwinner goes out to work he should take the coin from the toad's mouth and put it in his pocket and place the toad looking at the door, i.e. symbolically following him, helping him to earn money and when he returns home from work, he

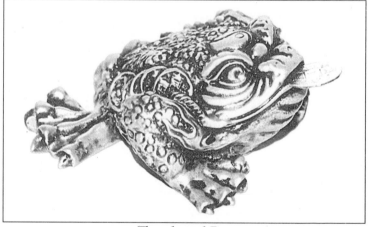

Three-legged Frog

should place the coin back in the toad's mouth and place the toad near the main door looking inwards, i.e. bringing in wealth all night. This means that if you want to use the toad this way you have to reposition it every day and every night. This method of using the three-legged toad is also quite alright, provided you don't mind the botheration of repositioning it twice daily! I personally find this method quite bothersome hence, I use the first method. It's your choice to follow whichever method you like. The important thing to remember is never to place the toads in the bedrooms, toilets, or the kitchen. Another important thing to remember is to clean the toad with a soft cloth periodically, so that dirt and dust do not accumulate upon the toad or on the coin in its mouth.

22

HORSESHOE

The horseshoe is considered a lucky charm in the West as well as in India ! The shape of the horseshoe describes the ideal land configuration of Feng Shui, hence it is considered a favourable shape as per Feng Shui too.

In India, people have traditionally considered the horseshoe as a lucky charm and used it by affixing it above their main door on the outer side, for protection and good luck. It is said that the real horseshoe which a horse has worn and which has been energized by the horses galloping, is very lucky ! If you happen to find such a horseshoe you can affix it above your main door on the outside above the door frame. Since the horse-shoe is of metal element avoid its usage for East and South-East facing doors. It is more useful for West, North-West and North facing doors.

The ideal way is to affix the horseshoe with its prongs pointing downwards as shown in the figure. A lot of people affix the horseshoe with the prongs pointing upwards. This is also not wrong. When the horseshoe is affixed in this way it is said to bring in good luck, but when it is affixed with the prongs downwards, it is said to even protect the house from evil spirits and negative energies! I personally have a horseshoe above the main door of my house with its prongs pointing downwards since many years, to create the protective energy for my house, along with good luck.

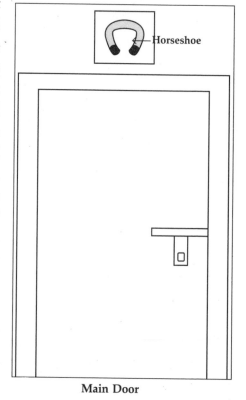

Main Door

SAU-THE GOD OF LONGEVITY

Sau is one of the three Chinese gods which are together known as Fuk, Luk, Sau. The God of Longevity is Sau and he is most popular as he symbolizes good health and a long and smooth life, free from sickness.

Sau is shown as an old man with a staff in his hand and the magical gourd is tied to the staff. The gourd or the Calabash is again an excellent symbol of longevity. The God Sau is not worshipped but is just displayed. The most suitable place to keep Sau is the living room and diagonally opposite to the main door. Please note, that there should not be a window or a toilet or the kitchen directly behind, or in front of him.

Sau

PAIR OF CRANES

After the Phoenix, the crane is the most favoured of all the birds as a symbol of good fortune. The crane is considered as the patriarch of all feathered creatures and is called the bird of immortality. It is symbolic of a long and smooth life and brings happiness and harmony into the home.

According to Chinese mythology, there are four types of cranes i.e. black, white, yellow and blue. The black crane is said to live the longest i.e. for 600 years.

The flying crane signifies achieving great honours and the crane gazing upwards signifies wisdom. If you display a white crane, it ensures harmonious relationship between the family members. Displaying a pair of cranes in the house is symbolic of the unity of the patriarch and the matriarch and the continuation of the family.

Pair of Cranes

The best location to place the crane is in the South which could bring you lot of opportunities and fame. If placed in the Northwest, it is favourable for the patriarch of the family. If displayed in the West Sector, it benefits the children of the family. It is not advisable to place the crane in the toilet or the kitchen.

SYMBOL OF LONGEVITY

The Chinese have used calligraphy widely for portraying different symbols. One such symbol is the symbol of longevity. The word which means longevity is a popular and auspicious word used in calligraphy. The symbol shown in the picture is not calligraphy but it is another version of the word which is more stylized. The longevity symbol not only symbolises a long life, but it also reflects good health and lots of harmony and happiness for the family members.

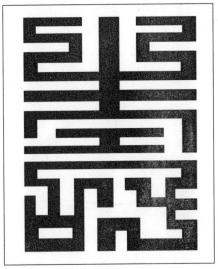

Symbol of Longevity

The symbol of longevity can be displayed in the bedroom to enhance the health luck of the patriarch of the family.

PAIR OF GEESE

One of the excellent symbols of love and romance is a pair of geese. The image of a pair of geese flying high is symbolic of unity and togetherness between the married couple. The geese are considered to be faithful creatures and hence portray undying love. The geese should always be displayed in a pair, neither single nor more than two. They should be shown as flying, and the best place to display the flying geese, is the South-West of your living room. The geese are regarded as a very good energiser for having a happy married life.

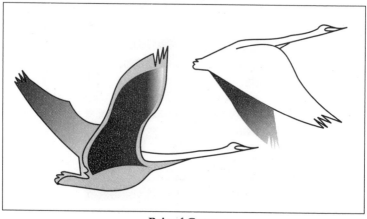

Pair of Geese

FU DOGS

Fu Dogs are mythical creatures of Feng Shui. They are regarded as protectors of homes. The Fu Dogs though they look like lions, are actually different. They

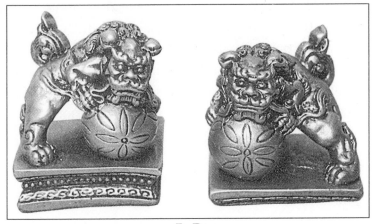

Fu Dogs

protect the house from negative energies. The Fu Dogs are suitable to ward off evil or people with bad intentions from entering the house. The Fu Dogs can be placed outside the main door. The pair of Fu Dogs should be placed at a high position.

28

PAIR OF LIONS

The lion symbolizes courage and bravery. According to Feng Shui, the lion is considered as a guardian protector to homes and other places. A pair of lions is especially used as a protection against evil spirits. It is mainly used for sacred buildings and temples. A pair of lions can be placed on either side of the door. These lions are generally shown with both their front feet on the ground. You can display a pair of lions made of ceramic outside your main door.

29

KUAN KUNG

The Chinese consider Kuan Kung as the God of War and also a God of Wealth. By placing the image of Kuan Kung in the house you are inviting powerful energies to protect your house. Kuan Kung is shown as sitting or standing or on horseback. But make sure that his staff and his sword are in place and you do not lose them since these are his two main weapons. Kuan Kung is symbolic of peace and harmony in the house. It provides protection for the Patriarch and brings prosperity for all. In a home, the Kuan Kung should be placed in the North-West corner and it should face the main door. The Kuan Kung should be placed high up as if he is watching the door.

Kuan Kung

In an office, you can display the Kuan Kung behind you. This symbolizes that you always have powerful people, behind you.

△ 30 △

(**THE CONCH**)

The conch is considered to be a suitable symbol to energise travel luck. It is especially effective for people who deal in overseas business and travel abroad a lot. The shell is one of the eight auspicious symbols found on the foot of the Buddha.

From Feng Shui view point, the shell attracts business luck from overseas. It is extremely beneficial for those who are in the export business or those who rely on foreign turnover for prosperity.

Conch

You can display a conch of about 6 to 8 inches in the house or office. If you are looking for fame or good reputation you can place the conch in the South sector of your living room. To enhance education luck the conch can be placed in the North-East area and if placed in the South-West it energises relationship luck.

31

SINGING BOWL

To improve the vibrations in the house a special tool known as the singing bowl is used. The singing bowl can be of various sizes and it cleanses the energies in the house. It is considered as an excellent tool for space clearing purposes. Using a singing bowl in the house improves the harmony among family members and the place becomes **yang**. It creates a state of **Yin** and **Yang** balance.

The singing bowl is a special bowl which is made of seven metals, i.e. gold, silver, copper, tin, iron, lead and zinc. All the metals used have a specific purpose and represent the sun, the moon and other planets.

While using the singing bowl it has to be placed on a cloth cushion so that the sound coming out lasts for a longer time. There is a wooden mallet to strike the bowl.

The procedure to use a singing bowl is to first gently strike the bowl at the rim with the wooden mallet. Then start rubbing the mallet at the rim in a clockwise direction. In this manner, you can make the bowl sing. At first the sound coming out could be flat and harsh. But gradually, as you get the hang of using it, the sound emitted will be softer and clearer. Frequent use of the singing bowl makes the energies purer and purer. It converts the auspicious **Chi** into sound that is calming and soothing.

Singing Bowl

TSAI SHEN YEH-GOD OF WEALTH

In symbolic Feng Shui, one of the most popular Gods that symbolize wealth is Tsai Shen Yeh. He is depicted as sitting on a tiger. His robe is shown as having a dragon motif which again is a sign of prosperity and good fortune. You can display the image of Tsai Shen Yeh in your living room. This prevents you from having bad luck and poverty, while in good times it brings wealth.

Tsai Shen Yeh

This God of Wealth should be placed in such a way that he faces the main door either directly or diagonally. TSAI SHEN YEH is a powerful God and is sometimes shown as carrying a symbolic gold ingot and a bundle of coins. In the other hand, he carries a staff with all the precious symbols. This God looks fierce but is relaxed at the same time!

Displaying the image of this God of Wealth in the bedroom is considered very inauspicious, hence display it only in the living room looking at the main door, preferably looking at it diagonally.

PICTURE OF PINE TREE

The pine tree is one of the favourite symbols of longevity. Even in the cold winter months, the pine does not lose its needles. Though there is snow all around the pine, the tree is not covered with snow. This shows its strength and fortitude. Displaying the pine tree in the form of a picture or landscape painting, signifies a long life full of personal achievements.

When the pine tree is shown along with bamboo and plum tree together, they signify true friendship which will last through thick and thin.

(MAGIC MIRROR)

Mirrors are used frequently as Feng Shui cures. The magic mirror is one of them. I have learnt to use it from one of my revered Gurus, the great Lillian Too. It is a simple mirror, which after it is cleaned and purified, attains certain attributes. The magic mirror can then be used for protection, for purification or for transforming negative energies to positive.

The procedure to use the magic mirror is as follows :

1. The mirror should be round in shape and should be big enough to fit in the palm of your hand. The mirror should also have a handle so that it becomes easier to use.

2. On a sunny day, hold the mirror in your hand and allow the sun to be fully reflected in the mirror.

3. Keep your eyes lowered while doing this, since the glare of the sun is blinding.

4. Tilt the mirror in such a way, that the sun's reflection in the mirror does not fall on you or anyone around you as this could cause burns.

5. The sun should be reflected in the mirror for a maximum of nine seconds. If you are unable to hold for nine seconds, even six seconds will suffice.

When this procedure is over, your magic mirror is ready. For space purifying purpose, you can move around with the mirror in all the rooms of your house. Then, immediately take the mirror outside and shine it at the sun. When the mirror is reflected in the rooms it captures the negativity. After each use, the mirror has to be held against the sun so that it becomes purified again and neutralizes the bad energy.

Magic Mirror

Similarly, in an office where there is lots of competition and if there are people bearing malice towards you, a mirror can be used. You can shine the mirror across the length and breadth and height of the room. This would capture any malicious intentions towards you and neutralize it. Then at the first opportunity, you make the face of the mirror reflect in the sun.

WINDCHIMES OF 5, 6 AND 7 RODS

Windchimes are an excellent source of enhancing good luck in the house. The number of rods in a windchime and the material by which a windchime is made are important. You are not supposed to hang windchimes anywhere and everywhere in a house. Their location is extremely important. The best place to hang a six-rod windchime is the North-West corner of your living room, since the governing element of this corner is metal. They are used to enhance good luck and also to reduce bad luck. A seven-rod windchime can be hung in the West zone of your house which is excellent for enhancing creativity, and children's luck.

If you want to deflect a poison arrow, you should use a five rod windchime as it also suppresses the bad luck. The five-rod windchime is especially useful for reducing the bad luck which occurs due to 5 yellows Annual Flying Star. In an Annual Flying Star chart, the location of the unlucky star 5 is the location of the 5 yellows for

Windchimes

THE VARIOUS FENG SHUI SYMBOLS FOR GOOD LUCK

that particular year. It brings extreme bad luck to the person using a bedroom or sitting in a location in the office which has the 5 yellows for that particular year, in that location. You can hang a five-rod windchime in the location of the 5 yellows to suppress its ill effects. The following chart shows the location of the 5 yellows in particular years. You can follow this chart and shift the five-rod windchime accordingly every year.

In the following Year	Five Yellow is in this area
2000	North
2001	South-West
2002	East
2003	South-East
2004	Centre
2005	North-West
2006	West
2007	North-East
2008	South
2009	North

CHINESE COINS

Hanging coins on the door handles is an excellent way to bring money luck into your home. You can hang three old Chinese coins, tied with a red thread or a ribbon on the door handle. This benefits all the members of the house. The coins should be hung on the inside of the door and not outside. Please do not go to the extreme and hang coins on each and every door of your house. Hanging coins on the main door is enough.

Chinese Coins

The use of Chinese coins to activate money luck is very effective. You can take three Chinese coins tied with a red thread and keep them in your purse or wallet. It symbolizes a continuous source of income for an individual. You can use three coins rather than four or five, since the number three itself is very auspicious.

These coins given as gifts to someone is wonderful. To energise the money flow these coins can be stuck on the front cover of account books and bill books or other books registering cash dealings. The coins can even be placed in the cash box in shops and at home. When sticking these coins on account book covers or on the inside of doors, always stick them with the **yang** side up, i.e. the side which has 4 chinese characters written, should be above and visible and the other side with the two characters should be below.

Another important use of coins is as a cure for certain Flying Star afflictions. The location in the house having star formations 3-2 and 2-3, which is called the bull fight sha, as the name suggests results in arguments and fights. The coins are used as a remedy for this defect. Ascertaining if such a combination of Flying Stars is present in your house and pinpointing its location, is beyond the scope of a book like this and forms the part of a professional and detailed Feng Shui audit.

CHIMING CLOCKS

Using musical clocks which give out soft tunes in the house creates good **chi**. But the sound coming out of the clocks should be pleasing.

Another kind of clock which is used as a cure in Flying Stars is the chiming pendulum clock. This clock preferably should be of metal and it should have a round metal pendulum. When the clock chimes, the sound coming out should be a metallic sound. Such a

Chiming Clock

clock can be hung in the area which is afflicted by the 5
yellows. The year and location of the 5 yellows has been
given in the Chapter on Windchimes. To find out the
place for the clock you can follow the given chart. The
sound of metal coming from the chiming clock is
effective in reducing the damaging effects of the deadly
5 yellows!

▲ ▲ ▲

C | AMAZING CRYSTALS - An Introduction

From time immemorial man has found beauty, power and mysticism in stones and crystals. Just as herbs possess healing powers, so do crystals. Crystals possess special energies which we can use to change our lives for the better.

The magic and mysticism of crystals is as old as man himself! It all began when the early races of humanity sensed that some special forces or powers were trapped within these crystals. These were first used as protective amulets to deflect negative or evil energies.

Just like the herbs, the crystals are also not inert. They may lie silently in the earth for millions of years waiting to be dug out, or rest in cupboards where we may place them, but they are really active and powerful things which possess energies that can and definitely affect our physical body, our luck and the environment around us.

Crystals are wonderful gifts from the generous Mother Earth, which we can put to good use to enrich our health, wealth and relationships. The best part is that they are not exorbitantly expensive, like some other precious stones. In the description ahead, you will read about many types of crystals, their special powers and uses. You will also know about the procedures of purifying and programming them with your specific aspirations for your benefit.   ▲ ▲ ▲·

D ‖ THE VARIOUS TYPES OF CRYSTALS

(CLEAR QUARTZ)

Clear Quartz is the most commonly used crystal in modern times. New age people have realized its value and potential and have made very good use of it. Clear Quartz is available and used in many forms like pendants or bracelets as personal wear or in the faceted ball forms for enhancing some areas of the home/office. Another use of clear quartz is to sculpt it in the form of a Shri Yantra. Ancient Indians considered the 3-dimensional Shri Yantras, hand sculpted out of real Quartz Crystal as a powerful tool to improve their lives.

Modern technology uses clear quartz crystals in radio transmitters and receivers as well as the computers to store and release information in the form of electromagnetic energy.

Reiki healers make use of quartz crystals as a healing device.

For protective uses, this stone is worn by a person as a pendant or used in the house in the form of faceted balls. It is also kept in the temple of their homes in the Shri Yantra form.

A quartz crystal pendant worn around the neck, increases psychism. Using it by placing beneath the pillow offers psychic impulses in the dream-form which is actually the language of the deep conscious mind. It also enhances peaceful sleep.

Crystal Pendant

Crystal Bracelet

Crystal Ball

(Clear Quartz)

Crystal Shri Yantra

(Clear Quartz)

PROCEDURE FOR PURIFICATION AND PROGRAMMING OF CRYSTALS

All crystals and stones should be purified and programmed before use. Crystals can record vibrations and before they reach you, they may have passed through the hands of the miners, workers, etc. So please purify and programme them all, before using them. I have found the salt water purification method, the best way to purify them.

The procedure is as follows :

Immerse the crystal in a glass full of water with four spoons of unrefined sea salt (common salt). Use a non-metallic glass for this purpose. Keep the crystal immersed in the salt water for at least one week. After a week remove the crystal from the salt water and throw away the salt water and then wash the crystal under flowing tap water. After this, keep it on a ceramic saucer and keep it in sunlight for around 2 to 3 hours. Early morning sunlight is better for this purpose. This is the purification procedure. After purification, your crystal is free of old vibrations, and is ready for being programmed with your personal programme. Crystals are programmed using images or thought forms i.e. a picture in the mind. The procedure of programming is as follows :

First decide what you want to achieve mainly from the use of the crystal, and then think of a very appropriate picture which describes clearly, what you desire. For e.g. if you want a promotion, you imagine a picture wherein you are sitting in the seat of the desired new designation, with a plaque describing your new position/rank kept on your office table. Don't forget to visualize yourself in the picture with a smile on your face. The smile is always desirable because it symbolizes satisfaction and happiness in the new situation. Another example is that if you want to use a crystal ball for the benefit of the full family you can use an image of the full family smiling and happy together with every one in good health and the ladies of the house wearing a lot of expensive jewellery. Such a picture is symbolic of happiness, togetherness, good health and wealth! These are just a few examples to guide you. It is you who must decide what exactly you desire, and then think of a really appropriate picture to use for programming your crystal. The actual procedure for programming is as follows :

After the purification, you must sit peacefully and practise forming a picture of what you desire, in your mind. Practise this till you are easily able to form and retain the image in your mind. This should be a single image, just like a photograph. Once you are ready with the image, get your crystal and keep it in your left palm and cover it with your right palm and then get the practised picture back into your mind, and retain it for about 5-10 seconds. This is the programming. Programming does the function of recording your desire, onto the crystal. It is believed that once programmed, the crystal channelises its powers to achieve the positive goal which has been programmed on it. The above-mentioned procedure for programming is generally what a layman can do easily, but readers who are well-versed in Reiki can go one step further and energise the crystal with Reiki (Positive healing energy). I had mastered Reiki years back from a Reiki Master and have been using it since then for my benefit as well as for ENERGISING all the Feng Shui cures and crystals that I use for my clients. I have had some of my readers telling me that there are some

Feng Shui consultants, selling their Feng Shui products and crystals at a very high price, citing the reason, that those have been 'energized' by them! I personally do mass energizing for the Feng Shui products and crystals, using Reiki healing energy absolutely at no extra cost. The products available with us are all energised, but we don't charge exorbitantly just because they are energised. Readers should not get carried away with all these tall claims of energizing because it is nothing very great, but just additional healing energy of Reiki used to make the Feng Shui cures and the crystals a little more effective. In fact a lot of readers who know Reiki themselves, can and should energise the crystals themselves using the Reiki energy. Reiki is universal healing energy. It is God's gift to mankind and comes absolutely free!

CLEAR QUARTZ PENDANT

The clear Quartz can be worn around a person's neck in a chain or thread, as a pendant. This helps in gaining more peace and enhances general luck of the person and increases psychism.

It is also said to possess such powers to protect the wearer from bad things and bad happenings. Before wearing any crystal, it must be purified and programmed. You may follow the procedure for the same as described earlier.

CLEAR QUARTZ BRACELET

The clear Quartz can be worn as a bracelet also. The benefits of wearing it this way are similar to the benefits gained by wearing it as a pendent.

CLEAR QUARTZ CRYSTAL BALLS

The South-West area of the house is connected to love, romance and relationships. This area has the earth element. The best way to energise this area is with the use of two genuine quartz crystal balls. The activation of the South-West corner of your bedroom with real crystal balls ensure harmony and happiness in relationships with your loved ones. If this is done in the living room, relationships within the whole family get enhanced.

If you want your daughter to get married, hang two crystal balls in the South-West corner of her bedroom as well as the South-West corner of the full house. Of course, the image used to program the crystal balls in this case, should be in accordance with the end result desired. The ideal image would be to visualize that your daughter is already getting married to a promising young fellow and she is smiling. The smile signifies that she finds happiness in the new bond rather than it being enforced upon her. In the same picture, you should also visualize yourself and your other family members adoring the newly-wed couple with gratifying smiles implying that you all are also happy with the marriage.

CLEAR QUARTZ CRYSTAL
SHRI YANTRA

Symbolic Feng Shui means making use of things that symbolise good luck. Chinese people use a lot of traditional Chinese cultural symbols for good luck. We in India also have our own lucky symbols and articles and we can make use of them for our benefit. The most powerful of Indian symbols is the Shri Yantra. The symbol of Shri Yantra is said to be very useful for acquiring good luck, peace, health and protection, etc. in the house.

The Shri Yantra has been in use for thousands of years in India. The Shri Yantra is symbolic of Goddess Mahalaxmi, the Hindu Goddess of Wealth and Prosperity!

The Shri Yantra in its most powerful form is described by the ancient Indians to be sculpted out of clear Quartz Crystal in a three-dimensional form in the right geometry as described in ancient literature. The Shri Yantra is also made in the two-dimensional form by engraving on a plate made of gold, silver or copper. But the three-dimensional form made out of real quartz crystal is said to be the most potent for bringing good luck and harmony to the house.

Ancient Indian literature describes very detailed procedures for pooja of the Shri Yantra to be performed, but I personally feel that doing a salt water and sunlight purification procedure to cleanse the crystal Shri Yantra and then keeping it in the pooja place of the house and just praying to goddess Mahalaxmi with a clean and pure heart is also sufficient, if you do not know the detailed procedures. There is also no need to do the programming of the Crystal Shri Yantra, only the purification in salt water and sunlight, and then the offering of prayers to Goddess Mahalaxmi, is quite sufficient.

It is important that the Shri Yantra should be made of real and genuine crystal of high clarity only. There are lot of fake crystals available in the market, so please be careful where you get it from. Genuine Crystal Shri Yantras are a little costly because the Crystal used to make them has to be a big, single and very clear piece, and also the Shri Yantra is to be hand sculpted.

It is said that in a house where the Shri Yantra is worshipped every day, there is always abundance of health, wealth and peace!

ROSE QUARTZ

Rose Quartz is pink in colour and is used to stimulate love and to open the Heart Chakra. To attract love, one can wear a heart-shaped pendant made out of Rose Quartz.

Rose Quartz crystal is effective for promoting fidelity in relationships and also for promoting peace, love and happiness.

Rose Quartz creates a soothing influence, and is very useful for calming the emotions. It is very useful for the healing of old memories and emotional traumas and scars in the minds of people, which may have occurred due to childhood abuse, neglect, separation or a desertion by a loved one. It also helps in warding off stress-related illnesses and mood swings.

Rose Quartz is a beautiful gift which lovers can gift to each other to promote fidelity. It is also a useful gift to children or anyone in need of sympathy and affection. Of course, the heart-shaped pendant should be used only for gifting to a lover or a spouse. Others may gift it in the regular pencil-shaped pendant form.

Rose Grape Bunch

Rose Quartz like any other quartz should be purified and programmed before use.

The Rose Quartz is generally available in pendants of the heart and pencil shapes and in the bracelet form. It is also available in the form of a bunch of grapes (Rose grape bunch) which is very useful to keep in the Southwest of the house or bedroom to enhance relationships with loved ones (spouse) or for enhancing romance or marriage prospects of unmarried girls in the house. Of course, the programming should be also done according to what is the desired objective.

SMOKY QUARTZ

Smoky Quartz is also a mood elevator. Natural Smoky Quartz absorbs and neutralises harmful influences and shields the wearer from harm. It is also worn as a grounding stone and increases our understanding of Mother Nature and the environment. It also helps to overcome negative emotions and depression.

This variety of quartz is not in great use today but was commonly used in olden times during prayers for healing.

AMETHYST

Amethyst is a purple coloured Quartz Crystal. It is as popular today as it was a thousand years ago. It is a marvellous healing crystal. The Greeks of olden times believed that Amethyst could prevent drunkenness.

Amethyst is a spiritual stone, it is a stone of peace. It has the power to control the various types of the harmful behaviour, to increase will power, to sharpen the memory and to make the immune system stronger.

When the stress of modern day life is too much and affects you adversely, hold the amethyst in your hand and let the soothing and calming vibrations help you unwind ! You may even permanently wear it on your wrist or around your neck in a chain or thread.

Amethyst is believed to help in calming an extremely passionate nature. Moreover, all emotional and mental problems can also be solved by Amethyst. It is also believed that Amethyst helps in protecting soldiers from harm and also helps to calm fears, raise hopes and lift up the spirits! It is said that keeping Amethyst below your pillow helps in removing insomnia and induces peaceful sleep and also promotes pleasant and healing dreams.

Amethyst helps in removing feelings of guilt and overcoming addictions like alcoholism.

Amethyst is also useful for people who travel very frequently and is said to protect the wearer from harm, sickness and robbery.

Amethyst is also used for increasing psychic awareness and to hone up the sixth sense or intuitive powers. Amethyst is used to enhance mental powers and is useful to relieve headaches, especially the headaches of people born on dates 3, 12, 21 and 30, i.e. number 3 people.

Amethyst like all other crystals should be purified and programmed before wearing. This procedure is the same as for the clear quartz crystal.

Amethyst is also said to be useful for those involved in litigation for improving the chance of ensuring that justice prevails! Amethyst is generally available in the pendant and the bracelet forms.

A powerful Taoist ritual, taught to me by one of my Gurus, the great Lillian Too, is the ritual to bring an errant husband back, i.e. to stop or prevent infidelity or in more simple language to stop or prevent your husband from having affairs with other women! The ritual involves tying a red string to the amethyst crystal and placing it under the bed, on the side that you sleep on. It is even more effective if you (the wife) sleep on the right hand side and your husband sleeps on the left hand side of the bed. I hope you have understood this clearly, the wife must sleep on the right side of the bed, the husband on the left side and the amethyst with red thread should be below the bed on the right hand side. You may tie it to the foot of the bed on the right hand side below you.

BLACK TOURMALINE

It is a black-coloured stone which is useful during situations causing emotional duress and situations of crisis! It is said to be a very useful stone for protection against negative energies of all kinds. It may be used to combat against, and protect from life-threatening ailments. The black tourmaline is a good guard against negative energies and it can also be used to ward off the evil spirits from the so called 'possessed people'. It is also believed to help the wearer to be free of fears and worries, and for soothing the central nervous system, to alleviate depression and nervous exhaustion. Black tourmaline is generally available in the pendant form as well as the bracelet form.

GEM TREE

A Gem Tree is a small tree made up of many types of semi-precious crystals and stones. It is multi-coloured and is quite useful to enhance the luck of the breadwinner of the house when it is placed in the North-West of the house. It can even be placed in the South-East of the house for enhancement of the general wealth luck of the house.

Gem Tree

▲ ▲ ▲

E LIMITATIONS

This book is meant for the common man to try to help himself in his various aspects of life like health, wealth, relationships, etc. The procedures and the methods described in this book are sufficient enough for small improvements to solve minor difficulties in life by energizing the house using symbolic Feng Shui, which is like vitamins of the medical science. A generally healthy person, without any serious or major illness, can improve his health with vitamins, but vitamins are not of much use in case of any serious or major illness, wherein a detailed treatment becomes necessary. This is the analogy I can give you. If you have any serious or major problem in life, a detailed FLYING STAR and EIGHT MANSIONS Feng Shui audit of your home and office becomes necessary. But always be on guard that you do not go about consulting any amateur or inexperienced consultant, just because he charges you less. If you have a serious problem in life, it is better not to be penny wise and pound foolish! Consult a really, really experienced Feng Shui Master who is an expert in Flying Star Feng Shui and Eight Mansions Feng Shui both! There is no substitute for experience. Remember, that a genuinely experienced Feng Shui MASTER is worth his weight in gold! His fees probably would be repaid many times over, by the benefit you stand to gain from his expert guidance.

Another important thing is that, only from long years of experience, does a consultant really know, what works well in Feng Shui and what doesn't because a lot of original Feng Shui literature in China was destroyed by one of the emperors during his regime, hence the first hand experience of the Feng Shui Consultant is of supreme importance. This emperor had made use of Feng Shui knowledge for his palace and strengthened himself, and did not want his detractors to benefit from it, and hence he got a lot of original books of literature destroyed, and circulated books with fake knowledge about Feng Shui. These kinds of books still find their way into the modern world. Though there are so many schools (systems) in Feng Shui, only experience teaches one as to what works best, under particular circumstances. Symbolic Feng Shui, strictly speaking, is only a part of traditional Chinese cultural symbolism. Really powerful Feng Shui lies in the advanced Eight Mansions Feng Shui and advanced Flying Star Feng Shui. Both these are too complex to be described in books. This precious knowledge can only be passed from the master to his totally dedicated students!

Earnest Request :

Please do not send your house plans or questions by post or e-mail or make queries on telephone as these cannot be answered due to the busy time schedule of Dr. Parakh. Please use the e-mail or tel. nos. only if you desire to consult Dr. Parakh professionally for a Feng Shui audit based on advanced Flying Stars Feng Shui and Eight Mansions Feng Shui.

F | HOW TO GET THESE ITEMS

It is very important to use only authentic Feng Shui products made of the correct material in the right way. There are a lot of spurious and cheap products available in the market. Please assure yourself that you buy them from the right places.

The co-author Mrs. Seema Parakh has a collection of these items. All products are made of the right material in the right way.

If you wish to buy some of these items, you may contact Tel. No 670 0911 or personally come to the address given below, to buy these items.

IMPORTANT NOTE : WE ARE BASED IN MUMBAI ONLY AND WE DO NOT HAVE ANY DEALERS OR BRANCHES ANYWHERE ELSE IN THE COUNTRY!

ADDRESS :

> Ground Floor, Classique Building,
> Gulmohar Main Road, Juhu Scheme,
> Mumbai - 400 049.

Imp. Note :

1. Timings -Morning 10. 00 a.m. to 1.00 p.m. and Afternoon 2.00 p.m. to 5.00   p.m. only.

2. Closed on Sundays.

3. Please do not call up on any other telephone numbers of the authors for inquiries regarding these items, call only on 670 0911 for inquiries regarding Feng Shui products.

Landmark : Junction of Juhu Lane & Gulmohar Road.

How to Reach :

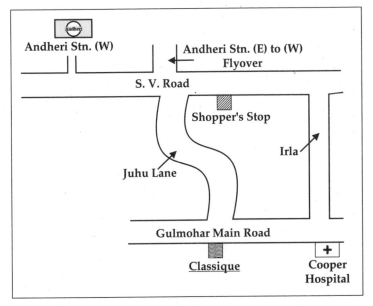

Outstation readers may please write to us, along with a self-addressed and stamped envelope. We will mail them the pricelist and they can, then, send a DD so that we can parcel the specified items, as per the order.

You can also get the pricelist by e-mail. Send your e-mails to nitinpar@rediffmail.com with "pricelist" in the subject line.

▲ ▲ ▲

	BEWARE OF SELF-STYLED
G	**AND INEXPERIENCED**
	FENG SHUI CONSULTANTS

After the huge success of my first book, (Feng Shui - 80 Golden Ways to Good Luck), some unscrupulous people, after reading the said book have started giving **consultation** or have started **teaching** Feng Shui. This is downright fraudulence and readers should be careful of such imposters! Some people feel that Feng Shui is only about placing a few things like wind chimes, crystals, frogs, etc. Nothing could be farther from the truth! All these products and symbolic Feng Shui itself, is a very basic thing and actually a part of traditional Chinese cultural symbolism, which is just capable of giving some relief in one's problems of life and this much a layman can do on his own, by reading my books! Really powerful Feng Shui is actually Flying Star Feng Shui combined with Eight Mansions Feng Shui. This system is very complex to be described in books and it deals with the time and space dimensions of your house! In fact it takes years of learning by a person of high intelligence level to master this powerful science. Professional guidance on Flying Stars from a highly experienced Feng Shui Master is very potent and capable of delivering <u>truly miraculous results</u>. More details of Flying Stars are described in point nos. 6 and 7 of the following chapter ie. Chapter 'H'.

Another message that I want to give my readers is that before you decide to take professional consultations from a Feng Shui Consultant, please verify his background and reputation, his level of knowledge and experience. Get from him the name of the FENG SHUI MASTER under whom he has learnt as well as the years of his discipleship. Find out how many years has he been practising Feng Shui professionally. Ask him for references of some clients who have taken consultations from him earlier. Right to information is your privilege and you must use it to avoid people duping you. Remember, that a genuine expert has nothing to hide and will whole-heartedly provide you with this information. Do not go about consulting someone who just claims to be an expert but actually may not have AUTHENTIC KNOWLEDGE and may lack the required LONG YEARS OF EXPERIENCE. Always remember the wise old saying that THERE IS NO SUBSTITUTE TO EXPERIENCE!

▲ ▲ ▲

H | DETAILS ABOUT PROFESSIONALLY CONSULTING THE AUTHOR

The author of this book 'SARVSHRI Dr. NITIN PARAKH' is a highly experienced and much sought after FENG SHUI MASTER, and if you wish to consult him <u>professionally</u>, you may contact him on any one of the following Tel. Nos. :

Tel. : 620 3900 (Mumbai)

Cellular : 98201 47625

e-mail : <u>nitinpar@rediffmail.com</u>

Notes :

1. The above Nos. are only for securing an appointment. <u>Please do not call up on these numbers,</u> for any other type of inquiries, or inquiries regarding any information in this book, etc. as they will <u>not</u> be responded due to constraints of time, because Dr. Parakh runs a very busy schedule of professional Feng Shui Consultations for his clients.

2. For professional consultations, you will have to take an appointment, generally 1 to 3 months in advance, as he is generally booked in advance for this much time, during any part of the year. He undertakes only 1 or 2 visits in a day, because he does not like to compromise on the time he gives to each place during a Feng Shui Audit. A professional Feng Shui Audit of even a small 3 BHK apartment generally takes around 3 hours, because he attends and

observes even the smallest detail of the house, and draws a sketch of the house, showing the required corrections and enhancements.

3. During a Feng Shui Audit, Dr. Parakh takes the date of births of all the residents of the family, especially the main earning member of the house, and works out according to Feng Shui astrology the <u>lucky and unlucky</u> personal directions for each person and then advises lucky sleeping directions and facing directions for each member of the family, for enhancement of their personal luck.

4. The various sectors pertaining to the eight life aspirations like wealth, health, relationship, etc. are checked up and wrong placements are corrected, and enhancement of sectors are advised, using methods described in this book, among other things.

5. The main door of the house is extremely important and whatsoever be the reasons, the main door has to be lucky for the main earning member of the family, based on his date of birth. This is absolutely important from the prosperity point of view. If such is not the case, its directional reorientation is sometimes advised, by Dr. Parakh, during the Feng Shui Audit of the premises.

6. Dr Nitin Parakh is India's leading authority on the subject of Flying Star Feng Shui. He has mastered this tremendously powerful science from the world's topmost authority, the great Master Joseph Yu, by learning under him **for many years**. Dr Parakh has passed Master Joseph Yu's practical exams and is one of the very few practitioners in

Asia to be given **official recognition** by Master Joseph Yu and Feng Shui Research Centre, Canada.

During a professional audit, Dr Parakh takes into account the year of construction of the house and checks the exact facing direction of the house. In Flying Star Feng Shui, the accurate direction checking is of supreme importance. Approximate directions are not useful. Dr. Parakh is a highly qualified and experienced Civil Engineer too, and his technical background is a value addition in checking exact directions using a Lo-pan or Engineer's compass. With this data he makes the Flying Star chart of the house, which is like a horoscope/kundli of the house. This chart when interpreted correctly by a knowledgeable and highly experienced master, tells precisely about the general luck of the house as well as reveals the secret of the lucky and unlucky locations/areas within the house! Dr. Parakh then advises the breadwinner of the house to use the luckiest area of the house for strong enhancement of his luck.

7. To improve the general luck of the house Dr. Parakh studies the general Flying Star chart and surveys the surrounding forms around the house and then advises how to enhance greatly, the lucky water stars and mountain stars. At the same time, bad star areas are cured with the use of special Flying Star Feng Shui remedies.

▲ ▲ ▲

I | DETAILS OF FENG SHUI COURSE CONDUCTED BY THE AUTHOR

A large number of people all over India have expressed their desire to learn the marvellous science of Feng Shui from Dr. Parakh. This overwhelming demand from all over the country was the result of the phenomenal success of Dr Parakh's best selling book, 'Feng Shui - 80 Golden Ways To Good Luck', which had endorsements from many eminent people, including the great **Amitabh Bachchan.** The said book is available in 8 languages! To satisfy this persisting demand to learn genuine Feng Shui, Dr Parakh has founded **FENG SHUI INSTITUTE OF INDIA.** Initially, the institute is conducting a prestigious CORRESPONDENCE COURSE. In this manner people from all over India, who have the desire to learn authentic Feng Shui, can do so very easily without leaving the comforts of their own home! This course is a unique and rare opportunity to learn AUTHENTIC FENG SHUI from the country's top authority on the subject.

This Course is actually a 3 in 1 course comprising BASIC + INTERMEDIATE + SEMI-ADVANCED – ALL THREE LEVELS IN ONE, comprehensive course. The course material is fully illustrated and all the concepts are very clearly explained. The areas where students generally get confused are thoroughly explained with lots of diagrams to facilitate clear understanding. In this course, Dr. Parakh has generously revealed a lot of information and secret techniques which are generally never revealed in books! The course can be completed within a minimum time of one month and a maximum time of one year, at your own decided pace. Presently, the course is available in the English medium only.

COURSE SYLLABUS

Form School, Basic Compass Formula, Symbolic Feng Shui, East house - West house formula, Eight Mansions Kua formula (**Pa-Chai**), The Luo-Pan, Empty line Danger Alignments, Time Dimensions, Introduction to Xuan Kong Feng Shui (Flying Stars), Time-taboos for renovation, Great Sun Position Formula and Annual Flying Stars. A test paper is attached at the end of the course and students have to answer it and send it to the Institute by Regd.Post. Students passing the test (i.e. securing a min. of 50%) will be awarded a **CERTIFICATE** by the Institute signed by Dr. Parakh himself.

HOW TO ENROLL

Students wishing to join the Course should apply on a plain paper with their name, address, Tel. No.and e-mail address if any, along with a DD for Rs.7000/- towards course fees, drawn in favour of 'FENG SHUI INSTITUTE OF INDIA' payable at Mumbai. Please note that the fee has to be paid in lumpsum and there is no instalment facility available. Please send your details on plain paper together with the DD by Regd. Post to the Institute's office at :

Ground Floor, Classique Building,
Gulmohar Main Road, Juhu Scheme,
Mumbai - 400 049.

Note : We have endeavoured to give all details about the course here, yet if you have any query, you may call on 022-670 0911 or write to us, or e-mail : nitinpar@rediffmail.com with 'COURSE' in the subject line.

REGISTRATION AND DESPATCH

On receiving the application and fees, your name will be registered as a student and an I.D. No. will be issued and the course material and your fee receipt will be dispatched by Registered Post or Courier to your postal address.

▲ ▲ ▲

NAVNEET PUBLICATIONS (INDIA) LIMITED

NAVNEET®

OFFICE ADDRESSES

Mumbai : Navneet Bhavan, Bhavani Shankar Road, Dadar, Mumbai - 400 028.
(Tel. 462 6565 • Fax : 462 6470)

Ahmadabad : Navneet House, Gurukul Road, Memnagar, Ahmadabad - 380 052 (Tel. 745 1000)

Bangalore : No. 98, 1st Floor, 6th Cross Road, 6th Main, Malleswaram, Bangalore - 560 003
(Tel. 346 5740)

Bhopal : Navneet Sadan, E7/728, Arera Colony, Shapura, Bhopal,
Madhya Pradesh - 462 016 (Tel. 278 544)

Chennai : 30, Shriram Nagar, North Street, Alwarpet, Chennai - 600 018 (Tel. 434 6404)

Delhi : 2E/23, Orion Plaza, 2nd & 3rd Floor, Jhandewalan Extn; Behind Videocon Tower,
New Delhi - 110 055 (Tel. 361 0170)

Hyderabad : 2nd Floor, Bldg. No. 3-2-331, Somasundaram Street, Secunderabad - 500 025.
(Tel. 621 7348)

Kolkata : Newar Bhavan, 1st Floor, No. 87, Chowringhee Road, Kolkata - 700 020.
(Tel. 223 2497)

Nagpur : Agge Apartments, Agyaramdevi - S. T. Stand Road, Nagpur - 440 018
(Tel. 724 411)

Patna : 1st Floor, 36-D, Sahdeo Mahto Marg, Srikrishnapuri, Patna - 800 001
(Tel. 204 921)

Pune : Sita Park, 18, Shivaji Nagar, Near Bharat English School, Pune - 411 005
(Tel. 553 6364)

Surat : 1, Shree Vallabh Complex, Kotwal Street, Nanpara, Surat - 395 001
(Tel. 346 3927)

Vadodara : F/1, Vaidya Vatika, Opp. Hanuman Wadi, Sardar Bhuvan Khancho,
Vadodara - 390 001 (Tel. 422 087)

SHOWROOM ADDRESSES

• *MUMBAI* • **Dhruvi Book House**, G/1, Mariam Manzil, J.P. Road, Opp. Navrang Cinema, Andheri (W) ✦ 677 7078 • **Haria Book House**, 20 B-C, Mahavir Bldg., Bhandarkar Road, Matunga (CR) ✦ 408 4964 • **Mahavir Stores**, Shop No. 4, Ajanta Apts., P. M. Road, Santacruz (W) ✦ 649 4457 • **Navneet Showroom**, Near Sharadashram, B. S. Road, Dadar (W) ✦ 462 6565 Extn:545

• *DOMBIVLI* • **Smart Romsons**, Station Road, Nr. Tilak Talkies, Dombivli (E) ✦ 861 143

• *AHMADABAD* • **A.R. Book Treasure**, C.G.Road, Near Municipal Market, Navarangpura ✦ 656 3020 • **Manpari Marketing**, Navneet House, Gurukul Road, Memnagar✦745 1000 • **Supreme Educational Gallery**, Rajasthan Hospital Road, Shahibaug ✦ 285 9151

• *PUNE* • **Anshuman Collections**, Shop No 6-A, Ashok-Vijay Complex, M. G. Road, Pune-1 ✦ 401 2664 • **Poona Automobiles**, 177/78, Laxmi Road, Near Belbaug Chowk, Pune-2 ✦ 445 2655

• *NAGPUR* • **Mangalam**, Shree Vithal Complex, Opp. South East Corner, Dhantoli Park, Abhyankar Road, Dhantoli, Nagpur ✦ 549 476

• *NASHIK* • **Mahavir's**, Dattatreya Darshan, College Road, Nashik ✦ 802 509/317 924

• *HYDERABAD* • **Glorious Enterprises**, 4-3-548/1, Shop No. 11, Need's Arcade, Bogulkunta Cross Road, Hyderabad ✦ 475 3219

• *GODHRA* • **Puja Enterprises**, Shop Nos. 1, 2, & 3, Unique Complex Basement, Prabha Rd., Godhra ✦ 02672-49497

• *BELGAUM* • **Aum Trading Corporation**, G-1&4, Radio Complex, Shivaji Road ✦ 422 678

• *DHARWAD* • **Indira Greetings**, U.C.B. Complex, Near Yemmekeri, Station Road ✦ 444 025